D1604529

TRANSPORTATION
in Different Places

Adrianna Morganelli

🌳 Crabtree Publishing Company
www.crabtreebooks.com

Learning About Our GLOBAL COMMUNITY

Author: Adrianna Morganelli

Publishing plan research and development:
Reagan Miller

Substantive editor: Reagan Miller

Editors: Kathy Middleton and Crystal Sikkens

Notes to educators: Reagan Miller

Proofreader and indexer: Janine Deschenes

Design: Samara Parent

Photo research: Crystal Sikkens

Production coordinator and prepress technician:
Samara Parent

Print coordinator: Margaret Amy Salter

Photographs
Alamy: © imageBROKER: pp4 (top), 12; © Design Pics Inc: pp4 (middle), 21: © Lyroky:

Getty: © Wolfgang Kaehler: p18

Shutterstock: © Stephen Bures: title page; © William Perugini: table of contents;
© M. Shcherbyna: pp4 (bottom), 16; © 1000 Words: pp5, 9, 13;
© Pius Lee: p7; © ben bryant: p8; © David Varga: p20 (bottom);

All other images by Shutterstock

Front cover: Motorboats carry residents and traditional gondolas carry tourists around the canals of Venice, Italy

Title page: Children in Vietnam are often in charge of taking care of the family's water buffalo. They often ride them to make them go where they want them to go.

Contents page: In Denmark, many people prefer using a bicycle instead of a car or a bus to move around the city.

Library and Archives Canada Cataloguing in Publication

Morganelli, Adrianna, 1979-, author
    Transportation in different places / Adrianna Morganelli.

(Learning about our global community)
Includes index.
Issued in print and electronic formats.
ISBN 978-0-7787-2014-0 (bound).--ISBN 978-0-7787-2020-1 (paperback).--
ISBN 978-1-4271-1655-0 (pdf).--ISBN 978-1-4271-1649-9 (html)

    1. Transportation--Juvenile literature. I. Title.

HE152.M67 2015   j388   C2015-903955-X
                                                    C2015-903956-8

Library of Congress Cataloging-in-Publication Data

Morganelli, Adrianna, 1979- author.
    Transportation in different places / Adrianna Morganelli.
        pages cm. -- (Learning about our global community)
    Includes index.
    ISBN 978-0-7787-2014-0 (reinforced library binding) --
    ISBN 978-0-7787-2020-1 (pbk.) --
    ISBN 978-1-4271-1655-0 (electronic pdf) --
    ISBN 978-1-4271-1649-9 (electronic html)
    1. Transportation--Juvenile literature. I. Title.

HE152.M58 2016
388--dc23
                                    2015026807

Crabtree Publishing Company

www.crabtreebooks.com   1-800-387-7650

Printed in Canada/112015/EF20150911

Published in Canada
Crabtree Publishing
616 Welland Ave.
St. Catharines, Ontario
L2M 5V6

Published in the United States
Crabtree Publishing
PMB 59051
350 Fifth Avenue, 59th Floor
New York, New York 10118

Published in the United Kingdom
Crabtree Publishing
Maritime House
Basin Road North, Hove
BN41 1WR

Published in Australia
Crabtree Publishing
3 Charles Street
Coburg North
VIC 3058

Contents

Our Global Community 4

From Place to Place 6

In the City 8

Out of the City 10

Climate 12

Goods Around the Globe ... 14

On the Water 16

Trains on Tracks 18

In the Air 20

Notes to Educators 22

Learning More.....................23

Glossary and Index 24

Our Global Community

The world is a huge place! In fact, people live in about 200 countries around the world. Each country is made up of many **communities**. A community is a group of people that live, work, and play in the same area. You are part of your **local** community. You and everyone else on Earth make up a much larger community—a global community!

snowmobile on frozen ground, Greenland (page 12)

GREENLAND

ALASKA (USA)

CANADA

NORTH AMERICA

U.S.A.

MEXICO

NORTH ATLANTIC OCEAN

delivery by bush plane, Alaska, USA (page 21)

PERU

SOUTH AMERICA

ARGENTINA

Staten Island Ferry, New York, USA (page 16)

Alike and different

Everyone in our global community is connected. Learning how people in different places live shows us how. This helps us understand how we are the same, what things make us different, and the ways in which we depend on each other.

Transportation is the movement of people and things from one place to another. In this book, you will learn about the different kinds of transportation people use around the world. The map below shows some examples.

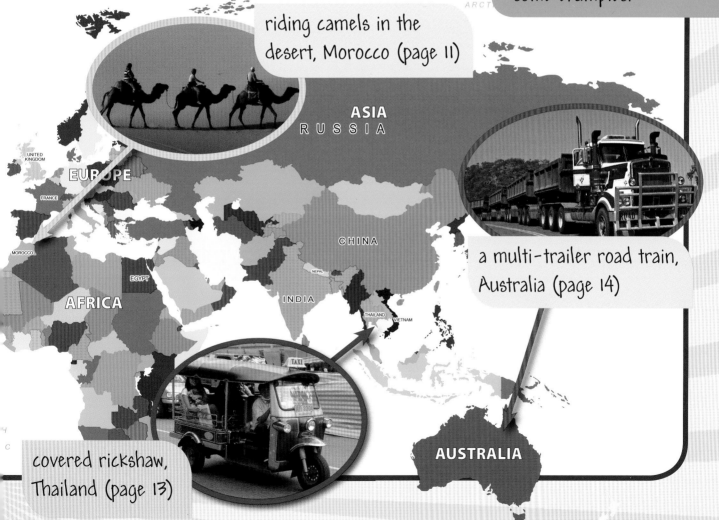

riding camels in the desert, Morocco (page 11)

a multi-trailer road train, Australia (page 14)

covered rickshaw, Thailand (page 13)

ASIA
RUSSIA
EUROPE
UNITED KINGDOM
FRANCE
MOROCCO
EGYPT
AFRICA
CHINA
NEPAL
INDIA
THAILAND
VIETNAM
AUSTRALIA

From Place to Place

People around the world use transportation every day! This is one thing we all have in common. People use transportation to visit family and friends, go to school or work, and go to stores to buy things they need. Sometimes people use transportation to travel to places far away, such as other cities or countries.

Planes help people travel long distances to connect with other people in the global community.

Many machines

People use different **vehicles** to get from place to place. Vehicles are machines that carry people and things, such as bicycles, cars, planes, and boats. Some vehicles are made to travel on land, while others are made to travel on water or through the air. People use different kinds of vehicles depending on the places they live and where they need to go.

In India, roads are crowded, so many people ride bicycles. These children ride in a vehicle called a cycle rickshaw to get to school.

In the City

The community a person lives in affects the kind of transportation they use. Cities, or **urban** areas, are communities where a lot of people live and work close together. People often walk or ride bicycles to get around. To travel farther distances in cities, many people drive cars, motorcycles, or other vehicles. Too many vehicles, however, can cause the roads to become crowded. The fumes, or smoke, from most vehicles also **pollutes** the air.

Roads in cities are usually covered with a layer of hard material called pavement. Paved roads are smooth to drive on.

Many people use the subway to get to school or work in Bangkok, Thailand.

Moving many people

To cut down on the number of vehicles on city roads, many cities around the world provide **public transportation**. This means transportation that moves many people at one time. Buses and **subways** are types of public transportation. A subway is a kind of underground train that travels on tracks. Buses and subways stop at certain spots along their **routes** to let people get on or off.

Out of the City

Rural communities are in the country, far away from cities. Most homes and buildings are spread far apart. People usually drive vehicles to get from place to place because it is too far to walk. Roads in the country are made of dirt or stones, and are often rough and bumpy. Many people in the country drive **pick-up trucks**, **off-road vehicles**, or tractors. These vehicles have tires that grip uneven road surfaces better than cars.

Tractors are vehicles used to move farm equipment from one place to another.

Today, most people cross the desert in vehicles, but in Morocco some still use camels. A camel's body is suited for travel over the hot, sandy, waterless land.

Surrounding land

Landforms, or the shape of the land, around communities can affect the kinds of transportation people use. In mountain communities, the land is on a **steep slope**. Sometimes there are only rocky paths instead of roads. This makes transportation difficult. In Peru, people often use animals such as alpacas and llamas to carry people and heavy loads down narrow mountain paths.

Climate

The **climate** of a place can also affect the kinds of transportation people use. Climate is the usual weather in an area. Nunavut, in northern Canada, has a very cold climate. Ice and snow cover the ground for most of the year. There are few roads in Nunavut. Many people use snowmobiles to travel over the snow and ice. A snowmobile is a sled with skis and a motor.

Greenland also has a very cold climate. Snowmobiles are a common form of transportation here, too.

During the rainy season in Thailand, people often use **motorized** vehicles called tuk tuks. These covered vehicles protect passengers from the wet weather.

Riding in the rain

Many places in warmer climates have only two seasons each year—a dry season and a rainy season. In parts of India, a lot of rain falls during certain times of the year. The rain sometimes floods the streets. People cannot walk or drive cars on the flooded streets. When this happens, some people use rafts or small boats to get from place to place.

Goods Around the Globe

Transportation is also used to move **goods**. Goods are things that can be bought or sold. They can be things that people grow, such as fruits and vegetables. Goods can also be things that people make, such as clothes and toys. Most communities cannot make or grow all the goods they need. Some goods must come from cities or countries outside the community.

In Australia, trucks called road trains are used to carry goods to far-away communities. Some road trains are so long they have 62 wheels!

Moving goods by truck

Trucks that have **trailers** carry goods from city to city. A trailer is a box that can hold a lot of goods. Some goods need to be carried in special vehicles. Foods that can spoil are carried in refrigerated trucks to keep them cool. Trucks that move animals, such as cows, have trailers with holes to provide air and special floors to prevent the animals from slipping.

tanker

Tanker trailers carry liquids such as gasoline and fuel oil. This tanker is delivering gasoline to a gas station.

On the Water

Boats carry people to and from places that are near water. In Italy, the city of Venice is made up of 117 small islands. Instead of roadways, the city is connected by waterways called **canals**. People that live there get around in their own small boats or on **ferries** called waterbuses. Ferries are used in many places around the world. Some ferries carry only people, while others carry people and their cars, too.

The Staten Island Ferry carries 70,000 people a day to and from New York City.

crane

Container ships carry goods packed into large metal boxes. Cranes move the containers to and from the ship.

From ship to shore!

Ships are large boats that carry people or goods over long distances. Ships bring goods across oceans and lakes, and along canals and rivers. Some goods need to be carried in special kinds of ships. Tankers are ships made to carry liquids, such as oil. Refrigerated ships called reefers are used to keep meats, fruits, and vegetables fresh.

Trains on Tracks

Trains move people and goods over tracks on land. Passenger trains carry people to different cities and countries. Some countries in Asia and Europe have high-speed trains. These trains run between major cities and move much faster than regular trains. A high-speed train connects the countries of England and France, which are separated by water. The train runs for more than 30 miles (50 km) through an underwater tunnel called the Channel Tunnel, or Chunnel.

The longest train route in the world is more than 6,000 miles (9,000 km) long across Russia!

Some goods require special kinds of cars. These tractors are carried on **flatcars**. The rounded tank cars are carrying oil.

Bringing goods to your community

A different kind of train moves goods between communities. Freight is a word used to describe goods being transported. A freight train can have hundreds of cars connected together! Each car is a container for goods such as foods, oil, animals, cars, and other items. Trains can travel over long distances and move more people and goods than cars or trucks. Fewer cars and trucks on the roads creates less pollution.

In the Air

Flying is the fastest form of transportation. Airplanes and helicopters are used to transport people and goods quickly over long distances. Passenger airplanes can carry hundreds of people at one time. Airplanes travel to places all over the world. Helicopters can carry only a few people, but they can land in areas that airplanes and other vehicles cannot.

Helicopters can be used to rescue people stranded, or trapped, on a mountain.

This airplane can fly up to 555 passengers between big cities, such as Paris, France, and Hong Kong, China.

These children are helping unload a bush plane that is delivering goods to their remote community in Alaska.

Large and small

Instead of passengers, some large airplanes carry goods known as cargo to different places around the world. Bush planes are small airplanes that are used to bring both people and goods to hard-to-reach communities, such as islands or rural areas. Bush planes have special parts so they can land and take off on water or snow.

Notes to Educators

Objective:

This title encourages readers to make global connections by understanding that even though people use different types of transportation depending on where they live, people everywhere use some form of transportation every day to travel near or far.

Main Concepts Include:

- transportation is necessary to move from place to place
- different kinds of transportation are used to move people and things

Discussion Prompts:

- Revisit the types of transportation described in the book. Connect each type of transportation to the climate or environment in which it is found. Ask readers how each type of transportation compares to their own experiences of travel? How are they the same? How are they different?

Activity Suggestions:

- Invite children to explore a form of transportation that is in their local community and another one from the global community.
- Ask each child to create a list or Venn diagram of the similarities and differences between their two chosen vehicles. Describe what each vehicle usually moves.
- Invite the children to explore some more and create a chart using pictures and words that include the following:
  - Transportation that travels by land
  - Transportation that travels by water
  - Transportation that travels by air
- Encourage children to give at least one example of something or someone that may use each mode of transport.

22

Learning More

Books

Hall, Margaret. *Transportation Around the World*. Heinemann Library, 2003.

Walker, Robert. *Transportation Inventions: Moving Our World Forward*. Crabtree Publishing Company, 2013.

Websites

www.sciencekids.co.nz/sciencefacts/vehicles.html
Learn some fun facts about different kinds of vehicles used for transportation.

www.primarygames.com/socstudies/transportation/transportation.htm
Explore this site for activities about different forms of transportation, and try your hand at some games and quizzes!

www.sesamestreet.org/parents/topicsandactivities/toolkits/groverand khokha/transportation
Watch the videos, explore different types of transportation children use around the world, and try out the activities with your family or classroom!

Glossary

Note: Some **boldfaced** words are defined where they appear in the book.

canals [kuh-NAL s] (noun) Human-made waterways for travel

ferries [FER-ee s] (noun) Boats that carry people and things across water

flatcars [FLAT-kahr s] (noun) Railroad freight cars without sides or a roof

local [LOH-kuh l] (adjective) Describing a thing close to your home

motorized [MOH-tuh-rayz d] (adjective) To be powered by a motor

off-road vehicles [AWF-ROHD VEE-i-kuh l s] (noun) Machines designed to drive over uneven landscape

pick-up trucks [pik-uhp truhk s] (noun) Vehicles with an open back, used to carry materials

pollutes [puh-LOOT s] (verb) To make dirty or unclean

routes [root s] (noun) Regularly traveled paths

rural [ROO R-uh l] (adjective) Having to do with the countryside

steep slope [steep slohp] (noun) A high incline, or slant

urban [UR-buh n] (adjective) Having to do with a city

A noun is a person, place, or thing.
A verb expresses an action.
An adjective tells us what something is like.

Index

airplanes 6, 20-21
animals 11, 15
boats 13, 16, 17
bus 9
climate 12, 13

goods 14, 15, 17, 19, 20, 21
landforms 11
public transportation 9

rural 10, 21
ships 17
subway 9
trains 18, 19

trucks 14, 15
urban 8
vehicles 7, 8, 10, 15